A Letter to Lynda

A Letter to Lynda
and Other Poems

Funso Aiyejina

MALLORY

Published by
Mallory Publishing,
Aylesbeare Common Business Park,
Exmouth Road,
Aylesbeare,
Devon,
EX5 2DG,
England

For a complete list of titles, visit
http://www.mallorypublishing.co.uk
e-mail: admin@mallorypublishing.co.uk

First published in this form 2006 by Mallory Publishing
Copyright © Funso Aiyejina 2006

*First published in 1988 by Saros International Publishers,
Port Harcourt, Nigeria, ISBN 1 870716 04 3*

ISBN 1 85657 106 8

Cover design © Mallory International Limited 2006

All rights reserved. No part of this publication may be reproduced, stored in a retrieval system, or transmitted in any form or by any means, electronic, mechanical, photocopying, recording or otherwise, without the prior permission of the publishers.

For

Lynda, Abuenameh and Ararimeh
Mother and Sons

With profound love

Mallory Classic African Writing
An Introduction to the Series

Mallory International is one of the leading exporting booksellers in the United Kingdom, and works particularly in Africa, where our customers include many Ministries of Education, Universities, and other institutions.

We have found from experience that many classic works by African writers are out of print, or no longer available, and this series is intended to remedy that situation, making available for ongoing distribution a range of titles, both fiction and non-fiction, which might otherwise disappear.

I hope you enjoy this book. If you do, and you are aware of another important title which could usefully be reprinted, please contact us. E-mail addresses and contact details can be found on our web site.

Julian Hardinge,
Chairman,
Mallory International

Acknowledgements

I am grateful to the editors of *Okike, Greenfield Review, Trinidad & Tobago Review, West Africa, Rhythms of Creation, Summer Fires, Penguin Book of Modern African Poetry, Ife Monograph Series on Literature and Criticism,* and *Ife Studies in African Literature and the Arts* where earlier versions of some of these poems have appeared.

I am also grateful to my past teachers, the several creative writers I have encountered in person and/or in print, school mates (especially members of "UWI Players," St. Augustine, who made me feel at home away from home in Trinidad) and, most especially, Lynda, who inspired the title poem and who has continued to be an enduring source of support.

Preface

A Letter to Lynda and Other Poems is a part of my attempt to comprehend our complex historical, cultural and official context as black people. I have chosen our experience of the slave trade (an original sin), the consequent monumental fission which this has caused between Europe/the Middle East and Africa on the one hand and between continental and diasporic Africans on the other, and our present always-coming, never-arriving dawns as the main sources of my central poetic metaphors.

One emergent constant in this exploration of our brutalized collective psyche is that although we remain the professional victims in other people's histories, such people have not always come from outside the castle of our skin. More often than not, the true culprits have been natives of our persons and cultures. They have been men and women with whom, as starry-eyed idealists, we shared dreams of the magic egg with which to banish poverty and all other forms of injustice from our midst.

In spite of the mangled omens bequeathed by our past and the horrors and frustrations which our present insists on making the legacy for the future, the ultimate creed which informs these poems is that we must resolve to celebrate the hardy hope of the desert cactus and the green dreams of oases. That, really, is our only option, if we believe in a better tomorrow.

Funso Aiyejina,
Ile-Ife

Contents

Mallory Classic African Writing	vii
Acknowledgements	ix
Preface	xi
A Letter to Lynda	1
And Today I Recall	6
History-Stretched…	8
Tenuously Airborne…	9
Seaspeaks	11
Once Upon a Time	12
Growing Up	13
As Men Melt…	14
When the Monuments…	16
May Ours Not…	17
The Learning Process	18
Let Us Remember	20
The Gathering Darkness	22
The Dialogue	23
Another Dialogue	24
And So it Came to Pass	25
Our House of Follies	26
Flowers of Hatred	27
Another Garden of Eden?	28
Mariatu: A Memorial	29
Reality, My Dear…	30
To Abuenameh (27 May 1984): In Celebration	32
To Abuenameh at Two	34
To Ararimeh (18 September 1986): Another Celebration	37
To Abuenameh at Three	38
To Ararimeh at One	40
After the Last Shot	41
Author's Profile	45

A Letter to Lynda

Dear Lynda,
    What is incalculably far from us
in point of distance can be near us.
Short distance is not itself nearness.
Nor is great distance remoteness...

    We who have been separated into one
by the troubled waters of the Atlantic
and united into two by the truths
of our common pasts,
we must learn with those who have travelled
the snail's trail with the tortoise
that those chased into rocky limits
must grow
to pelt boulders at their assailants;
seas reflect only objects above their surfaces,
none but divers
may perceive secrets buried in their wombs;
those abandoned to the mercy of water
must practise to swim like fish
or   perish.

    I who have wandered across mountains
and across valleys in search of history,
I have recognized myself in the scars
of those who have survived the misdeeds
and the greed of our common ancestors:
ancestors who grovelled after beads
after mirrors and after liquid fires
with which to prop up their sagging genitals,
ancestors who fashioned crude tools
with which they punctured our radiant morning
dew-drops

so that today our twin summer noons
embrace the same mad ocean of our related pasts.

    Now I deepen my soul into the inkwell of history
and write to you
across the virulent Atlantic pages of our separation;
I sing of you: muse with the full-moon face,
the magic egg of my many journeys,
native of the twin islands of Trinidad and Tobago,
the terminal colon that stands your archipelago
in anticipation of future explications.

    Lest we should forget so very soon
why progenitors of thunder-wielding ancestors
now chew grass beneath our ghettoes' dirt heaps,
let us remember our related betrayals:
the chains the whips the sea the sun,
let us remember your stray islands
bracketed between two visible Americas
and appositioned to an invisible Africa
and a far Far East;
let us remember so we may never forget:

    Antigua,
where if you ask what the King's chamber pot
has in common with the Princess who,
virgin no more, came on honeymoon in the sun,
you will be told by a proud black guide
that they both shared Clarence House
on Shirley's Height which overlooks an English harbour
far away from the shores of England;
where too, at Carnival, men reverse ancestral taboos
as mere mortals whip bull-horned masquerades
to the tune of God save the Queen.

    Barbados,
the nearest to and the furthest from Mother Africa,
where the apoplectic froth and foam
of Bathsheba Beach
mock the complacency of the populace
(Bathsheba, concubine to King Solomon,
Bathsheba, Mother of the Lion of Judah,
I celebrate your anger;
if the Pacific so desires, let it stay peaceful,
it was never baptised with the blood of slaves)
and at Bridgetown's Harbour,
overseen by Admiral Horatio Nelson,
you can watch beach boys dive
for coins tossed by sun-hunters
from aboard the Jolly Roger
into the dark muck of the harbour,
and when the winner surfaces with a large grin,
he is greeted by the silver glare of cameras:
masks over the faces of the offspring of past massas.
(But some day, them beach boys going to dive
deep down
deeper down than them tourists' copper coins
into the womb of the past
to resurrect skeletons
that will name the unacknowledged
whose sweat built these islands in the sun;
but until then,
let them tourists keep on tossing them coins
in the name of God, the Father,
God, the Son, and God, the Holy Ghost);
    Amen.

    Amen to Grenada,
(the youngest cousin of Cuba; Cuba, the gonad
of our thunder). Amen to Grenada

where the little people of a little place
have shown that to be grenade-shaped
is not enough
for those who wish to say no in thunder
from under...

    Guyana,
(the home of Pat, the widow of our Walter),
Guyana, land of failed leaders
and evaporating hopes;
we await the fulfilment of the thunder in your clouds.

    Jamaica,
gateway for Jah, the King of Kings,
where we went to the supermarkets
and returned with nothing for supper,
a nation under siege from itself,
a mecca where not even the gods are safe
as macho-men replace their manhood with guns
and advance the background sound of war
in their reggae to the front doors of their lives,
a haven where the failures of Man
have led the women to invite the Sea
into their thirsting wombs.

    St. Lucia,
Fair Helen that is fair no more
as redeemers of every persuasion
go dim once they become popular
and the fires of your fire-eaters are no match
for Soufriere's spit-fire and the lightning thunder
that heralds the hurricanes into Castries.

    Trinidad and Tobago,
the last of the archipelago,
a land muddy with the rust of several pasts,

a nation where the leaders start every race
as loud and clear
as the cascading waters of Maracas
but soon grow slow and devious like the Caroni river
which, navigable no more, teams up with the Orinoco
to turn the blue of the sea
into the brown of barren deserts.

    But above all,
I celebrate the one who says that in spite of all,
let there be a new beginning.
I will strap her like a diver's goggles
and go in search of the clues
to our future imperfect
so that, as the Niger flows into the Atlantic
that washes the early-morning face of the Caribbean,
we shall flow together to create new lives
who will not swing between two extremes
like strung-up hammocks
still only when dormant;
they will learn neither the language
of the ancestors who sold us
nor that of those who bought us;
they will learn only the language
with which the land communes with the sea
so they will grow to know
if one conspires to offer them
on a silver platter to the other....

    Extend
my warm regards to Mum and Dad
brothers and sisters and our mutual friends.
May history preserve us together into the future.

    Fondly yours,
    Funso

And Today I Recall
(for Edward Kamau Brathwaite)

I

And today I recall your islands'
bright beaches whose white sands
lure sun seeking souls
into the blue catacombs of passion,
where the greed of some
and the sweat of many
alchemized into profits for a few...
where too remnants of our people
live their life-sentences on bare pebbles
ruled by strange curren-ts-cies
as they vacillate
between God the creator
and Columbus the discoverer,
between Christ the meek
and Castro the rebel
and between a sea and a sky
whose twin infinities
mirror the eternity of our wait
for warriors from another life....

II

We who are born of rivers
must learn with our cousins
who have survived the turbulence
of oceans and the spasms
of racists with colour-blind sperm
(in a world where history has become a myth

and the fourth-of-July the only reality)
that tourists stretched out to tan
are no new christs on crosses,
decrepit boats that sail in bad weather
are wont to dream of storms
and that those who have lived to tell
of the touch of fire and the taste of ashes
must remember to frame and hang up
the potent moments of their lives
on the lighted portions of memory.

History-Stretched...

History-stretched between ancestors
and new world cousins,
I count our sins of blood
and our crimes of eternities
by the wavelashes that shatter the calm
of our sun-framed fortunes.
I contemplate your holiday resorts into
    mosaics of silhouette boats
    that sit safe in still harbours
    to await the arrival of auctioneers,
    luminous dusk-glow that stays the mind
    on echoes from primordial nightmares,
    shadows that cast shadows
    to map out white sea breakers
    into mastsails that once floated ships
    pregnant with our ancestral limbs
    and details that accentuate details
    to whip our past into permanent
    scars on the skin of our present pains...

Tenuously Airborne…

I

Tenuously airborne and anticipative
like one on the verge of a still-born sneeze
I came
over the gulf which separates us into one
into this present which yields hyphenated-names.
From the rockhills of memories
from the giant question mark
on the conscience of the world,
across land across seas across phobia
I came
to the wavecrests of Sans Souci
to the last of the sea-periods
that slow motions into near stops
to re-chart centuries of foot-steps
that came chained
and to watch waves chase men
and men chase waves
in games they play by the beach
as the sea seeks cracks into the day
and men seek peep-holes into their yesterdays.

From the rivers that sliver the continent
into this sea that imprisons your islands
I came
to watch history spray rockcliffs white
and shock those who believed the Queen dead
but forgot to sing Long Live the King….

II

This sample graffiti from the leprous walls
of Toco's derelict lighthouse:
*John Pool Ricky Annie Won't Be Here Again
So F... Off—*
so they cursed and so they painted
to leave later callers to see and to wonder
who they were, why, where they went
and with what winds they left....

If only they had taken down the danger signs
chased out the bats and the darkness
and camped in and around this ancient point
once the suicidal lure of defeated Arawak warriors
and the abrupt death of drunken merchant ships,
and, from here, given new lights to a new world!
If only.   If only they had.

Seaspeaks

Early o'clock footprints that rupture virgin beach
    sand
waves that break sand heaps
on the edges of barren shores
ears that stand in anticipation of hurricanes
and volcanoes
hearts that beat to the music of violent
    backlashes
and faces blinded silly by the silver glare of a sun
on a shuttle service between peaks of sea
    breakers
are the rhythms that beat on the seams of your
    sea-dreams.

Behold your regiments of waves on the wait
uncertain whose commandments
and whose intentions to obey
in these islands of tensions
where cheap black deaths
have replaced cheap black labour
as brothers fight to outdo each other
in the race to install new whip-wielders;
behold the relics the tides have resurrected
from the depths of our history's sleep-chamber
unto the corridors of our hopes
to teach beach boys with a new anchorage
in a sea that is new no more
to learn to float fleet
like mangrove roots in the swamps,
live on the sea,
not walk into its depths
in search of ends to present pains.

Once Upon a Time
(*or* The Bar Beach Show, Lagos)

Once upon a time
men were wise enough
not to charge bats
for crimes committed in broad daylight
or to expect drift wood to stay dry on waves;
they knew too that only true equals
should be allowed into the square
to wrestle for prizes,
that you do not burn a house
to destroy its mice,
you do not crush a head
to kill its lice,
you do not employ a mountain
to crack a walnut….

But today, see how we execute bats
tied to the stakes, backs to the lagoon,
for crimes committed in Broad (day) Streets….

Growing Up

Growing up, we slept in dark windowless rooms
on mud-beds hard as rock, mats wet as dew drops
on sheets tattered like storm-ravaged banana
 leaves
we dreamt of fleet-footed seven-headed monsters
fast devouring the ground behind our escape
towards flooded ravines and unbridged rivers
and rafters shaped into blood-sucking tarantulas
holding ceremonial parades on our petrified
 torsos....

But we always awoke to mother's knowledge of
 nightmares:
our insurance back into phantomless
 slumbers....

Not so any more;
ominously, like the epidemic-laden noon-heat
of a resident tropical harmattan season,
history herds us towards mined futures
as our benevolent guardians personalize our
 fortunes
into coded vaults
sky-rocking caps
and epaulet-laden shoulders;
our grown-up streets are paved
with decimated oppositions
and our market places are overseen
by daylight squanderers
who, come evening time, usurp our few surviving
 fireflies....

Today, we need no nightmares to caution us
to fear the living, not the dead.

As Men Melt...

As men melt into the shadows of caves
and the distances of far away farms
while their wives lie without persuasion
to cover for their poverty
during the tax man's visit
Adamu, disciple of the full moon
garnishes our deserted village square with
    questions:

> *Do men fear the dew on footpaths so much*
> *that they abandon their unharvested farms?*
> *Can we step on cool earth on a hot day*
> *without first throwing cold water ahead?*
> *The axe that feasts on honey from rock crevices*
> *does it not wear twisted edges for adornment?*
> *The penis that is fearful of the vagina's darkness*
> *will it ever father a child?*

Abandoning questions, an ancient voice chanted:

> The hawk has a grace of flight
> it is our fear of its claws that makes us jump
> at mother hen's frantic squawks...
> you can bend to touch your pre-noon shadow
> but you cannot step on its distant head...
> the shrine may withstand the weather
> it is the priests, crowned with frail feathers
> that we must learn to distrust, always.

Embracing their future, our ancestors-in-ascent
    descanted.
But our nights are none the wiser
in spite of the moon and the stars.

When the Monuments...
(for Walter Rodney and Ngugi wa Thiong'o)

When the monuments to our past
grow mouldy with neglect
and our dew-drops of change
are squashed on the altar of state security
we awake to the knowledge that
pebbles lodged in muddy ponds
must grow muddy with time....

Now that our messiahs have chased our dreams
from the sacred corners of our hearts
into the blind alleys of our ghettoes
where they proceed to slaughter them
before our astonished imagination
summoning history to witness their feast
it is time we rejected those who have
severed the link between prayers and miracles
those who mock our needs with giant signboards
which proclaim only fairy-tale projects
and those who make us build the podia
on which they stand to salute our misery
on every anniversary of the revolution.

May Ours Not...

May ours not be like the story
of the Ear and the Mosquito;
but if it is, remember, o plunderers
the Mosquito's eternal vow of protest.
For we shall become the lice
forever in your seams,
ant-heads that even in death
burrow deep into the flesh,
chameleon faeces that cannot
be wiped clean from errant feet,
and regenerating earthworms
that multiply by their pieces.

If there is no rainbow in the sky
we know to create one
by splashing water in the face of the sun.
When sleepers protect their ears with their hands
mosquitoes bite at their legs
to awaken them into their broken pledges.
If treasure hunters disturb our Orukwu rockhill
thunder will break
behind our tongues of lightning
like arrows in flight….

The Learning Process

Starry-eyed before M.T.D. Ajakpo, the HM
(may the good gods bless him
with a comfortable spot in the here-after)
we recited nation-building alphabets
with innocent zeal
believing in the incredible trinity
after which our school was named...
to spell a long, difficult, and foreign river
we were taught to write to the rhythm of
m i double-s i double-s i double-p i....

But our youthful months mounted their aging years
to give birth to these decades of men
who only double the M in their Mine
and the I that defines Self-Importance;
Kilimanjaro: the snow-capped African mountain
    of our Atlas
has metamorphosed into 'Kill man Jah an' row'
    at last!
the almighty Jah killed the good natured Mallam
and rowed a fatuous Alhaji to a landslide victory....
Hurrah for democracy;
Amen to the mockery of the race.

Starry-eyed before Albert, the infidel
after he had changed both his name
and his nature to Yesufu, the believer
and practiced to wash his turbulent sex
five times daily
so he could become potent,
we chanted endless *La illah illa Allah*...

Alhamdu li 'llah...
singing gospel songs to no other god but Allah, praising
Him
alone
not knowing then, until now
that in truth and in practice
Lai lai Alamu o le dede la
Eewo Orisa!
The gods themselves forbid it
that Alamu, the peasant
should suddenly become rich and important
unless, of/f course, he joins the harmattan chorus of
one nation
one con/tract/or
join them in looting the treasury dry
flash an immaculate smile at inquisitive journalists
and shoot an agile and impeaching fore-finger
in the face of our God.

Let Us Remember
(for Dayo Babatomi, a fellow traveller)

We who have listened to silences abort
before they were diagnosed
as stream-flow of seminal blood
out of tune with monthly cycles...

we who have collected clouds
that eventually burst into storms
and left us aghast as our crops
became feeders to ocean bound streams...

we who can point to fragments of kites
and strands of thread
entangled on high voltage cables
as evidence of our dispersed dreams...

we who can smell the stench of dead pigeons
by the waterless fountains of our memorial squares
as evidence of the death of the *in*
in our independence...

we who have danced at festivals of arts
while cripples from new tribes
prance around on stilts
and trample our pre-harvest fields of crops to death...

let us remember
how men of parliament vacationed the electorate
bandits demanded donations with which to refill
treasuries they had looted into family pots
and power dissolved the people...

let us remember
how men, feline skunks, bury their insides sub rosa
forgetful of bamboo groves whose sacred flutes will grow
to play the tunes they plant in beach sand
and manifest the ugly lump on the king's crowned head
which he forbids his barber to proclaim before the people.

The Gathering Darkness

Darkness gathers around us; again
like waves heading for unfortified forts
locusts hovering over unharvested fields
and phantoms polluting ponds of hope
to make men wish for words
stronger with every utterance
with which to invoke green dreams
populated with full and fearless rivers
active volcanoes mummifying the brazen sins
accruing from our redeemers' bill-board promises
into the seventh bowel of the earth....

But there is no more room for dreams in this place
here where we pray for plateaux of flaming flowers
over which our eyes may roam eternal
but are re(a)warded with rocky deserts
over which elemental monsters preside,
where too we ask for harbours of rest
but are herded into cathedrals of betrayals....

Where then to find salvation
now that those who should mend the broken fences
around our wilting dreams
would rather mutilate our cactus-willed hopes
and abandon us to our rosaries of pains?

The Dialogue

Perched on his Balcony of Pleasures
beside a range of gifts
the King asked the Poet
who stood below to pay homage:
"How are my people faring
On this most beautiful day?"

The Poet stretched his ostrich neck
and readied the traditional trick
of "We thank our God and our King
by whose twin grace
our heads still sit on our necks…."
But the lie choked his weaverbird throat
forcing him to answer:
"Your Royal Highness
we, your people
are too hungry
to see
the beauty in this or any other day;
things are getting worse by the day
as we await
the fulfilment of the better days
you promised us this time last year
same promise we have heard
from the echoes of every voice
that has ever occupied that throne
upon which you sit and fart."

Livid, like a seven-barrelled thunder
the King withdrew with his gifts
and the poet starved with the people.

Another Dialogue

When the people raised their voices
to the mansions on the hill-crests
overlooking their dreams
guarded by armoured dogs and errand guns
and said in unison:
"Your Most Benevolent Victors, Husbands of our Votes,
we, your people are hungry; our pots are empty
and our dreams are barren…",
the Victors sent down their hirelings to tell the voters
to go feed on their votes!

Just so!

When the people replied saying
how they had used their votes
to bring them their Fortunes,
one of the most victorious of the victorious
laughed
aloud
and announced to the world
that they were victors
long before the people voted.

Ours is a land of many miracles;
Always has been.

And So it Came to Pass

And so it came to pass
many seasons after the death of one Saviour
that a new crop of saviours, armed with party
programmes, came
poised for the poisoning of our Atlantic reservoir
they sought out the foxes in the family
to whom they gave thirty pieces of silver
in local and foreign exchange
for the secrets of the passage-
ways into the castle of our skin....

Men we had taken for fearless warriors
as protectors of our secret recipes
suddenly turned crabs, carapace and all
shedding shame like water from duck-backs,
seeing sideways beyond the good of all
to the comfort of selves;
with divination bags of tricks
slung over arrogant shoulders
they crawl over our dreams
under the cover of moonless nights
sidestepping traps, destroying hopes,
they turn our green August of rains,
of showers with which to persuade crops
towards harvest-circles
around whose fire we would have exchanged
happy tales of toil
into an orgy of furious flames....

And so it came to pass
that our saviours have given us a gift of tragedy
for which we are too dumb-struck to find a melody....

Our House of Follies

There is magic in every word, in every act
known to preservers and perverters of truth alike.

When those elected to read between the lines of our dreams
falsify the realities of our daily lives
before our starving children,
give us flaming, wailing cities
in response to our wish for fantasy streets
emblazoned with bright human laughter,
and sustain us on instant formulas and expired promises,
let it be known that, again, the chameleons —
paintmasters with the avaricious eyes —
have been re-enthroned on the high altars
of our model democracy;
with their prehensile tails drilling
for the buried treasures of our desert,
they wag their long smooth tongues
at our dwindling green forests;
global eyes glowing with a percentage of several contracts,
they who should starve with us on our empty grain measures
feed fat on the mintmaster's pot of dye
and emerge the grandmasters of every ceremony,
disciples and apostles adept at manipulating fingers
to suit any and every rally,
extinguishing earlier consciences like match-flares
in the face of a raging storm:
master-builders erecting new gas-chambers
wherein they delouse expert forecasts
to add new tiers to our House of Follies.

Flowers of Hatred
(For Odia Ofeimun)

With soldier ants in our undergarments
slow worms in our entrails
and snares before our every step,
they advise that we should be grateful for little mercies
for ours is the Kingdom of Tomorrow....

But they forget that at their last state banquet
on the anniversary of our Kingdom of Chance
at Abuja: our Project Oliver Twist
alias paid contract-fees and giant promissory signboards
they had served our tomorrow as their dessert
and, ever so often, bequeath nothing to us but blood:
the cold blood of death, not the warm blood of birth....

Let us, therefore, descend into Dreamland
from whence to bring forth flowers of hatred
with which to counter the vulgar xerox culture
which they demand that we embrace
like greying creepers on dying trees.

Another Garden of Eden?

Clad in their regulation glory
with star epaulets on their cultured shoulders
battle-ready like arena bulls
the Generals are here again
to steer us
out of the depths of our nightmares
with multiple promises of green valleys
by whose clean, slow, winding rivers
we may plant our long grains of hope
and watch them grow into golden harvests;
they promise too to cut us a new path
straight and smooth
through our malarial forest of false prophesies
to lead us into a new Garden of Eden….

Another Garden of Eden?
With green-eyed serpents in its grinning foliage?

Mariatu: A Memorial

GRANDMOTHER
you whose riddles matured into mellow hopes
you who brewed dream-wines of patience
with which to soothe the volcanic temper
of the insolent youths of our moulding village,
nothing remains of your legendary patience now
but an unmarked mound: foot-mat for the elements:
reminder to all who dream of possibilities at night
but awake into nightmares at daybreak
to seize the dawn in their visions with body and soul
as men would the orgasmic moment of their manhood
so their green future will not yellow into brown drought
their sunsgold will not be translated into fixed deposits
in the rosy cheek-banks of old new champions
from the provinces: bats masquerading as owls:
blind to their faults in the day, marauders at night.

Reality, My Dear...
(For L. Q.)

As the professional victims in other people's history,
our imagination should sing of rivers
in whose mirrors we can behold green futures,
of seas on whose islands dreams can procreate
and of oases
with whose water we can resuscitate
our wilting hopes;
but rocks are the contents of our inheritance:
boulders in whose dark wombs ancestors sheltered
from the long impersonal spears of hired raiders
and pebbles on which others skidded
in their bid to escape from the pain-fields of another life....

Rather than seek anchorage where there are no harbours
and buoyancy in sandy shallow waters,
fearing painted oceans
like those for whom ships are metaphors of bondage,
let us seek courage in memory and pointers in a new history
like stallions, galloping and multiplying
across mountainous terrain,
ceaselessly appearing and disappearing
like the crests of tidal waves:
an eternal light, restless and dashing
like a dancing mask
whose feats cannot be comprehended
by those who stand rooted to any one spot....

Reality, my dear, is being your captive soul
under the mellow gaze of an island moon
or by a river bank, in the absence of islands:

together, like two shadows stealing towards hope
to rendezvous with the foaming white questions
breaking ecstatically at the coral feet
of our dawn dreams of green pastures,
impatient for the simple truths
beyond contrived songs of praise,
original like the elements,
strident like the tangled contents of our past.

To Abuenameh (27 May 1984): In Celebration

Even in this age of the fire next
and the flood never
as vultures gather
on the crumbling walls
of our resistance
to descend at dusk
on our always-coming
never-arriving dawns,
we rejoiced at your arrival
in the month of May
when the Mayor of Rain
endows the going-out faces
of our mountains
with His greenest garments of hope....

He comes to resurrect us into a new future
past these afternoon showers of decrees
and commandments
he to whose midnight calls we must respond
promptly
like the exemplary brides in the parable
needing no siren
to awaken them into the epicentre of destiny....

Golden harvest of our interlocking histories
form over our present continuous
may the harmattan rage
and not crack your laughter
may the waves surge
but deposit only blessings at your feet

may the scorpions under your rock of rest
die
victims of your weight.

And may you live long
to better and bury us: your parents.

To Abuenameh at Two

I

The anniversary of your future has come around again
coinciding as it does with their Children's Day
when, with tongues coated in synthetic honey
they don their ceremonial garb
whether they be elected, selected, or decreed
bring out their full arsenal of rainbow-coloured
promises in custom-made packages
parade uniformed children as spectacles
to massage their bloated egos
and force our heads, dead set
in the direction of their development plans
designed for the repossession of our receding horizon:
their magic yeast for the resurrection of our dead dough....

But do not be deceived by men who are long on promises
but short
on delivery
like the penial boast of impotent men with access to power
men whose smiles are as false and as lucrative
as the golden teeth of pilgrims newly returned from Mecca.
Protect too your cherished balloons
from their outstretched hands of friendship
studded with the balance of the thorns
out of which they fashioned the crown-on-the-cross.

II

If birthdays must be celebrated
let them return us to futures too sublime
to be captured by our instant Kodak culture
like that afternoon when we went walking

down our neighbourhood cul-de-sac
and you asked for a gift of the yellow butterfly
which had performed to the applause of your
    innocent eyes
and I said no: you must not imprison beauty
no matter how innocently
let beauty as truth roam freely
or that other afternoon in the zoo
when you saw and wanted a lion for a toy
and I said no: an uncaged lion among men
invariably causes death by mauling
as in the dying days of the Lion of Judah
Emperor Bokassa in Bangui
Idi Amin in Uganda
and Mobutu still in Zaire....

Instead let me plant a cactus in your name
so you may grow to know the meanings
of parables about creativity in adversity
and learn too never to obey them
when they lead you as they led us
past green valleys and luxuriant forests
to the very edge of a desert precipice
and command from the safety of their stations
that you should take a giant step forward
into a golden future.

III

No, we will not dissuade you from the No
you have acquired so early in your life.
Why should we when there are so many lies
to which you must learn to say No

as amiable champions from the provinces
perfect the art of asking us to haggle
over how best to share the meat of an ant
when in their armoured backyards
with high walls posted to shut out our death throes
elephants are tethered in readiness for their
        breakfast?

To Ararimeh (18 September 1986): Another Celebration

Together, let us salute the cactus:
Crown Prince of the desert
whose defensive hostility
mirrors the future of the graffiti
on our dawn-wall of change:
strange beauty
born out of deprivation
distinguished
like a beacon on the horizon
beaming hope
to lost desert travellers,
step forward
with your numerous species
and tribes
to be proclaimed
the totem of our struggles....

Pathfinder and pathpointer
I pluck your scarlet bloom
to fashion garlands
with which to decorate him
and the many others
for and about whom I sing
and in whose dreams
I have elected to reside
long after we have celebrated
the demise of the evil ones
who have pitched permanent tents
on the shores of our oases.

To Abuenameh at Three

I

Again, as we join you in celebrating the flow of life
inherent in the anniversary of your birth
we make bold to invoke the sanctity of hope
and raise songs to the names and voices of the few
who point us always in the direction of good health....

But can we sing in earnest
without first confessing to the cob-webs of despair
with which they seal the path of the cacti
which alone sign-post the trail to moon-bathed oases
and the bloom of our future foretold?

Even if the stories about our genial generals
are not all true in "every material particular"
can we doubt the pain from the giant nails
driven into the palms of our hearts
by drunken robots from fortified stables
hell-bent on arresting the dreams in our heads?

II

As long as there are no rains in sight
to restore good health to our wilting crops
we cannot dream the dreams of the complacent.
Not now that your anniversary month of May
which should endow our fields of germinating grains
with the green colour of hope
spins only strange tunes of more pains
condemning us to traverse a universe

of deciduous forests stripped skeletal
into flaking six-fingered desert forms:
a prelude to the dreaded harvest of sand.

III

If somehow we survive their plots and blasts
should they despatch their regular operatives
or resurrect dormant informers among us
with strict orders to infiltrate our thoughts
with false grins of previous acquaintance
and seek out the meanings of our allusions,
rather than equivocate like men caught in the act
we must seek eloquence in the truth of the poet
and unveil the duplicity of the many image makers
who hawk the General's *Close-up* media portraits
as if *Macleans* smiles are the same as clean hearts.

IV

As you grow older by this day each year
remember
always
that the nightmare they spread across the face of our sleep
is only a moment of darkness
that we must not allow to blind us
before dawn when we shall rise again and again
intent on painting new dreams on our walls of hope.

To Ararimeh at One

September hosts the day we must remember
as that on which you came forth into our life
bubbling with the magic of another harvest
in the midst of their resolve to dismantle our dreams
and decree us to tend their post-retirement farms
farms which they irrigate
with rivers diverted from peasant plots
to boost the interests
on their ever-ready-never-red bank accounts.

In view of the interlocking realities of our traumatic history
the anniversary of your day is today a trans-Atlantic story
told before maternal cousins ingathered in the house of hope
built on the half-a-plot piece on the Belmont slope
but now without Mister Quamina, its builder:
the last patriarch whose up-front gift of a silver dollar
chronicled the imminence of his death
and the certainty of your birth.

As you take your first faltering steps
forward into a future of fluctuations
untouched by the conflicting details of our history
and the motives behind private and public intentions
we promise no miracles for the year 2000:
that magical year of our promise-spinning warlords;
we offer only the wonders of metaphors
in the popularity of the people
in pre-consolidation communiqués
in this, our continent of "I, Sergeant-Major-General..."
or in the psychology of the Cedrosian's guard dogs
who bark only at African visitors
in spite of the *one love* slogan of the new Alliance
and the *all o' we is one* of the previous National Movement.

After the Last Shot

Does the fire that consumes the king and his palace
ever remain the exclusive sorrow of his household?
Where does the town turn when the kingmakers demand
the beaded crown and the staff of office
when a new king is named?
What will the new eat if not the old?
What will he eat?

> the child who over-turns his noon meal
> because it's too small
> will surely taste hunger
> before the chickens come home to roost….

*Give us weight, the burden of the elephant
to stay firm on earth.*

The men who walk with their manhood
between their emaciated thighs,
the dogs that stand with punchless howls
and frail tails between their hinder limbs,
the limp he-goats that tease the she-goats on heat,
whose masquerades are these
whose head-gears have descended to their feet?

> masquerades who stay out for too long
> will surely return home with exposed toes
> crabs that sleep carelessly
> become the doomed companions of the flood….

*Give us lightness, the pride of the eagle
to escape adversaries.*

A waterfall….
a waterfall cannot be a fall if it does not fall,

its music cannot rise without its falling water,
unless the torrents tear through the checking craters
they can never descend to the foot of Orukwu
to water the baked farmlands
and open the gate for the promise of tomorrow.

> Put past flames past your tender mind,
> the rods that catch Sango's stray tongues,
> can they ever catch the god himself?
> Become, therefore, the god's own goddess
> and strike with your pent-up-hope
> if this be your day and your hour
> for how many past heart-breaks
> shall we continue to recall
> and how much of the water of this Niger
> can we drink before we die?

Give us weight for stability
and wings for mobility
give us voices for words
that will not sound vacuously
like war drums in a deserted village,
let ours not be like the decorative front-piece
that opens unto a filthy backyard.

> But let us float
> above the smouldering flames of our time.
> Let us float
> above the guilt-ridden gales of our age,
> this age of deaf-mute adults
> and talkative infants,
> this time of public promises
> and private retrievals.
> Let us float
> like two copulating butterflies

      atop a mid-day heap of cow dung
      intent on giving new beauties
      to a world gone berserk with ugliness....

For except by refilling
how else and how best
can we make full
an empty Go(ur)d?

Author's Profile

Funso Aiyejina is a literary and cultural critic, poet, playwright, and short story writer. He was born in Ososo, Edo State, Nigeria, and grew up in Temidayo Camp, a remote village near Ondo, to which his parents had relocated as migrant cocoa farmers. He is a graduate of the University of Ife (now Obafemi Awolowo University), Ile-Ife, Nigeria (BA); Acadia University, Wolfville, NS, Canada (MA); and The University of the West Indies, St. Augustine, Trinidad and Tobago (PhD). He taught for many years at the Obafemi Awolowo University before relocating to Trinidad and Tobago where he is a Professor in the Department of Liberal Arts, The University of the West Indies, St. Augustine.

A Letter to Lynda and Other Poems (1988), his first book of poems, won the Association of Nigerian Authors' Poetry Prize in 1989. It was hailed as "a memorable epistle" and as a "major new collection from a major new poet from whom we will hence demand only greatness" (Afam Akeh, *Daily Times*, Wednesday, August 9, 1989).

Since *A Letter to Lynda and Other Poems*, Aiyejina has published *The Legend of the Rockhills and Other Stories* (1999), which won Best First Book (Africa), Commonwealth Writers Prize, 2000, and attracted reviews from Canada, India, UK, Nigeria, and Trinidad and Tobago.

Kofi Anyidoho, Chairperson, Regional Judging Panel for Africa, in announcing the book as the winning entry for the Commonwealth Writers Prize 2000, had the following to say:

In The Legend of the Rockhills and Other Stories, *Funso Aiyejina draws as much on his considerable powers as a poet, as on the aesthetics of verbal art of his mother tongue. The result is a work in which the English language is constantly transformed and endowed with fresh powers of articulation. Not a single one of these stories seems to have been written in a hurry, merely to 'fill up space.' A coherent collection with a constant integrity of content, style, and artistic poise.*

T. Vijay Kumar, reviewing the book in India, affirms:

Ideologically and stylistically, Aiyejina's stories gesture towards Achebe, Soyinka, and interestingly for the Indian reader, to R. K. Narayan. Aiyejina's employment of irony rather than polemics, his even-handed treatment of tradition and modernity, and his use of proverbs as the repositories of communal wisdom, are strongly evocative of Achebe's writing. (*The Book Review*, XXIV. 4, April 2000: 20)

Tanure Ojaide, in *World Literature*

Today (74:3), concludes:

> The Legend of the Rockhills *may be Funso Aiyejina's first collection of stories, but it displays maturity of thematic exploration, experienced craftsmanship, and compelling narrative techniques.*

And Lakshmi Subramanayam writes: *Sharply etched, the writer's ironical, quizzical eye juxtaposes different worlds colliding against each other...* and concludes: *The collection of stories, though written in a deceptively simple style emerges as a perceptive, ironic unveiling of oppression and corruption, balancing realism with optimism"*

(*Hindustan Times*, March 2000).

In reviewing Aiyejina's second collection of poem, *I, The Supreme and Other Poems*, Jean Antoine-Dunne asserts: "Funso Aiyejina's writings span a life lived in Africa and the New World and celebrate the web of connections he has found therein ...

(*Metro Eireann* July 2005).

Aiyejina's writing career started during his undergraduate days at the University of Ife when he wrote a number of radio plays, which were performed on WNBS (Ibadan) and Radio Nigeria (Lagos), and had one of his short stories broadcast on BBC. His first stage play, *The Character Who Walked Out On His Author* (2004), has been performed in Trinidad, Nigeria, and Jamaica. In a response to the manuscript, Niyi Osundare describes *The Character Who Walked Out On His Author* as

A really fascinating work of the imagination (and that is not a cliché), the play brings to the fore the relationship (visceral, cerebral, psychological, mythical, social...) between author and character, creator and the created, cause and consequences. The author is anything but dead here. If anything, s/he has been summoned to the dock to be rudely but poignantly interrogated by a figure from the figment of his/her imagination. Here the created is posing questions which challenge, sometimes frustrate, the ostensibly supreme intelligence of the creator. One destined to a life between covers has burst through her/his prison and out-travelled its gaoler.

Aiyejina's short stories and poems have been published in a wide range of journals, including *Africa Update, Crab Orchard Review, Either/Or, From the Horse's Mouth, Greenfield Review, Isala, Ife Monographs on Literature and Criticism, Okike, Opon-Ifa, Toronto Review, Trinidad and Tobago Review*, and *West Africa*, and have been included in a number of anthologies such as *African Radio Narrations and Plays, Literature Without Borders, Rhythms of Creation, Summer Fires, The Anchor Book of African Stories*, *The Fate of Vultures*, *The New African Poetry* and *The Penguin Book of Modern African Poetry* where he has been described by Gerald Moore and Ulli Beier (editors) as "one of Nigeria's finest satirists" (413). His work has been translated into Russian, German, Urdu, and Hindi. His literary successes have earned him entries in *The Companion to African Literature* (2000), *Contemporary Authors* (2002), and the Online Contemporary Africa Database, http://www.africaexpert.org.

Aiyejina is the editor of *Growing in the Dark (Selected Essays of Earl Lovelace)* (2003), *Self-Portraits: Interviews with Ten West Indian Writers and Two Critics* (2003), and co-editor of *Caribbean Literature in a Global Context* (2006).

www.ingramcontent.com/pod-product-compliance
Lightning Source LLC
Chambersburg PA
CBHW020022050426
42450CB00005B/600